# The Remarkable Bunny Bakery

Written by Suzanne Marie

Illustrated by Emily Anne Hickman

Paperback:
The Remarkable Bunny Bakery


Paperback
First Edition: 2024

Printed by IngramSpark in the USA

A Cozy Day Books Press book

Written by Suzanne Marie
Book Cover by Emily Hickman
Illustrated by Emily Anne Hickman
Interior and Cover Design by Victoria Lynn with The Glory Writers www.glorywriters.com
Edited by Abigayle Claire with The Glory Writers

"Therefore comfort each other and edify one another, just as you also are doing."

-1 Thessalonians 5:11

"Let each of you look out not only for his own interests, but also for the interests of others."

-Philippians 2:4

"Be kindly affectionate to one another with brotherly love, in honor giving preference to one another;"

-Romans 12:10

BAKERY
Open
Sweet
Sweet treats & Hot Drinks
Welcome

A long time ago in a quaint little town there was a remarkable bakery.
It was owned and operated by two bunny sisters.
They made elaborate, delicious desserts and coffee drinks to warm the soul and brighten the spirit on any given day.

Snickerdoodle was in charge of baking and decorating.

A perfectionist at heart, she would work long dedicated hours to create fanciful pastries.

Her sister Hazelnut, loved concocting warm wonderful drinks—mochas, coffees, hot chocolates, and teas, great for sipping by the fire with a good book or conversing with a friend.

However, owning a bakery was a lot of work. Snickerdoodle toiled and fussed over her desserts. She had a passion for baking, but was beginning to grow weary of the endless hours.

Bunny Sisters
Coffee Co

Hazelnut, on the other hand, loved making and serving coffee alongside her sister's wonderful treats. She always took time to hear her customers' stories, hardships, or jokes. She would offer a listening ear and a kind word to all who wanted to share.

Snickerdoodle began to wonder, Why does Hazelnut never seem to tire? She always seems happy and content.

As she thought about this, she remembered a verse the sisters had been taught a long time ago.

"And let us not grow weary while doing good, for in due season we shall reap if we do not lose heart."

And let us not grow weary while doing good, for in due season we shall reap if we do not lose heart.
Galatians 6:9

Snickerdoodle, observed her sister, and she began to realize that maybe there was more to running a bakery than just endless hours of perfecting desserts. Yes, it was important to bake and bake well, but it seemed just as important to care for every customer who came in.

As the days went by she watched, looking for a way to help.

Tips

A border collie came in everyday with the same story about losing one sheep and then finding him again. He was excited, loud, and silly, which made her laugh.

A lonely squirrel talked about trying to find enough food to store for the coming year.

A beaver family told them of the repairs they had done to their home because of a mudslide.

Everyone had a tale to tell, or a success to celebrate, or a hardship to convey. She watched Hazelnut kindly listen as if everyone was her best friend.

Snickerdoodle wondered if there was even more good they could do if they worked together.

And then, one day it happened–a chance to do more.

As Snickerdoodle was filling the pastry case, a raccoon and her three children came in.

They looked cold and bedraggled. The mother took her time looking at the desserts and prices. She finally pulled out one small coin, enough for one cupcake.

It was her childrens' birthday, but there was only enough money for one pastry to share.

As they left, Snickerdoodle asked her sister about them. Hazelnut explained that they lived on the edge of town. Hard times had fallen on them and they couldn't afford food, resorting to eating out of the neighbor's garbage.

This broke Snickerdoodle's heart. There had to be more they could do. Both sisters put their heads together and came up with a plan.

They loaded cakes, cookies, and bread on a little cart to send to the family.

Snickerdoodle and Hazelnut rushed through town with the goodies, hoping to have an impromptu party for the little raccoons.

FLOWERS
We're Open
Sweet Treats
BOOKS
Hugs and Hot Cocoa
A Penguin Christmas

It was such a joy watching their faces when the food arrived. They all felt such gratitude. Snickerdoodle's heart was as full as theirs.

It was then she realized that being generous is what truly makes life sweet.

The next day, the sisters set up a little table in the shop for customers who couldn't afford a pastry or hot drink. And every day they blessed someone with a listening ear and a treat.

It wasn't about perfection. It was about the heart. And indeed, it was a remarkable bakery, because the sisters were remarkably kind.

The End

To Jonathan and Jessica who love bunnies and baking ~ S M

To David Franklin whose heart to shepherd and care for those around him has been a great inspiration in my life on how to love and serve well ~ E H

Printed in the USA
CPSIA information can be obtained
at www.ICGtesting.com
LVRC100739241024
794668LV00010B/45

* 9 7 9 8 3 3 0 4 5 6 3 5 2 *

Colours

# Comparing Colours

Nancy Harris

Heinemann

www.heinemannlibrary.co.uk
Visit our website to find out more information about Heinemann Library books.

To order:
Phone 44 (0) 1865 888066
Send a fax to 44 (0) 1865 314091
Visit the Heinemann Bookshop at www.heinemannlibrary.co.uk to browse our catalogue and order online.

Heinemann Library is an imprint of Capstone Global Library Limited, a company incorporated in England and Wales having its registered office at 7 Pilgrim Street, London, EC4V 6LB – Registered company number: 6695582

Heinemann is a registered trademark of Pearson Education Limited, under licence to Capstone Global Library Limited


First published in hardback in 2009
First published in paperback in 2010


Edited by Rebecca Rissman and Sian Smith
Designed by Kimberley R. Miracle and Joanna Hinton-Malivoire
Picture research by Tracy Cummins and Tracey Engel
Production by Duncan Gilbert
Originated by Dot
Printed and bound Leo Paper Products

ISBN 978 0 43119300 7 (hardback)
13 12 11 10 09
10 9 8 7 6 5 4 3 2 1

ISBN 978 0 43119304 5 (paperback)
14 13 12 11 10
10 9 8 7 6 5 4 3 2 1

**British Library Cataloguing in Publication Data**
Comparing colours. - (Acorn plus)
535.6
A full catalogue record for this book is available from the British Library.

**Acknowledgements**
We would like to thank the following for permission to reproduce photographs: ©age Fotostock p. **9** Right (Vstock); ©Alamy pp. **10** Top Right (Robert Tunstall), **11** Right (ephotocorp), **13** Bottom Left (Vick Fisher), **14** Bottom Right (blickwinkel); ©Corbis pp. **5** Top Right (DLILLC), **14** Top Right (Frank Lane Picture Agency/ Chris Mattison), **19** Right (Christophe Boisvieux); ©Getty Images p. **18** (Travel Ink); ©istockphoto pp. **11** Bottom Left (Marisa Allegra Williams), **13** Top Left (Steve Mcsweeny), **15** Right (Sam Lee), **17** Top Left (Matthew Thompson), **21** Right (Michael Sacco); ©Photos.com p. **5** Bottom Left; ©Shutterstock pp. **4** Bottom Left, **19** Top Left (Philip Lange), **4** Bottom Right (Péter Gudella), **4** Top Left (Cameron Cross), **4** Top Right (Daniel Gale), **5** Bottom Right (Voznikevich Konstantin), **5** Center (aaaah), **5** Top Left (Supri Suharjoto), **6** (Cynthia Kidwell), **7** (ANP), **8** (Lezh), **9** Bottom Left (javarman), **9** Top Left (Kathryn Bell), **10** Bottom Left (Joanne Harris and Daniel Bubnich), **10** Left (Maxim Tupikov), **11** Top Left (RexRover), **12** (Joanne Harris and Daniel Bubnich), **13** Right (Stephen Inglis), **14** Left (Sebastian Duda), **15** Bottom Left (Eric Gevaert), **15** Top Left (Ronen), **16** (Kristy Batie), **17** Bottom Left (Morozova Tatyana), **17** Right (Igor Grochev), **19** Bottom Left (Nick Stubbs), **20** (kd2), **21** Left (Jonathan Heger).

Cover photographs reproduced with permission of ©Shutterstock: black (Eric Gevaert), blue (Gordan), brown (Monster), green (Martin Nemec), orange (Francisco Amaral Leitão), red (Jorge Cubells Biela), purple (Clarence Bowman), white (Tischenko Irina), yellow (Florin C).
Back cover photographs reproduced with permission ©Shutterstock: frog (Cynthia Kidwell) and tiger (ANP).

The publishers would like to thank Nancy Harris for her assistance in the preparation of this book.

Every effort has been made to contact copyright holders of any material reproduced in this book. Any omissions will be rectified in subsequent printings if notice is given to the publisher.

# Contents



Some words appear in bold, **like this**. You can find out what they mean in the picture glossary on page 22.

# Colours in nature

There are many colours in **nature**.
These are some of the colours in nature.

orange

red

purple

white

yellow

# What colour are things in nature?

Are all things in **nature** one colour?

Are some things in nature many colours?

# Plants

Plants are many colours. Plants have many parts.

Some plants have leaves. Some leaves are red. Some leaves are yellow. Some leaves are green and blue.

Plants have stems. Some stems are yellow. Some stems are purple. Some stems are red and green.

Some plants have flowers. Some flowers are red. Some flowers are black. Some flowers are blue and yellow.

# Animals

Animals are many colours. Animals have **body coverings**. Some animals have feathers.

Some feathers are brown. Some are green and white.
Some feathers are purple.

Some animals have scales. Some scales are green. Some scales are white. Some scales are purple, orange, and yellow.

Some animals have fur. Some fur is orange.
Some fur is brown. Some fur is white and black.

# Rocks

Rocks are many colours.

Some rocks are red. Some rocks are green. Some rocks are purple and white.

# Soil

**Soils** are many colours.

Some **soils** are brown. Some soils are white. Some soils are orange and yellow.

# What have you learned?

Things in **nature** are not always the same colour.

Some things in nature are one colour.
Some things in nature are many colours.

# Picture glossary

**body covering** outer layer, such as skin or scales, that protects an animal

**nature** the world around us. Plants, animals, rocks, water, and soil are part of nature.

**soil** part of nature. Soil is made out of dead plants and tiny rocks.

# Words to know

**camouflage** the colouring of an animal or plant that allows it to blend in with its surroundings

**colour** the property of an object that depends on the light that it reflects

**environment** the surroundings or conditions in which a person, animal, or plant lives

**feather** the flat, partly hollow body covering on the body and wings of a bird. Feathers help some birds to fly.

**fur** the hair that grows on some animals for protection, camouflage, and temperature control

**habitat** the natural home of an animal or plant

**scale** tiny, flat plate growing from the skin of an animal for protection

# Index



## Note to parents and teachers

### Before reading

Talk with children about colours. Explain that there are many different colours in nature, and that each colour has a name. Use a colour wheel or other simple colour chart to name each colour. Then, ask children to make a list of the colours they can see. After they have completed their list, ask children to share their results.

### After reading

Turn to pages 6 and 7. Ask children to compare the images, and ask why they think the animals might have such different appearances. Encourage them to think about the kind of animal that might need to hide from predators. Then, ask them why they think the tiger has stripes. Discuss the concept of camouflage, as defined on page 23.